THIS IS AN APOCALYPSE CONFIDENTIAL BOOK
PUBLISHED BY APOCALYPSE CONFIDENTIAL PRESS
www.apocalypse-confidential.com

First Printing, July 2023

Book design by Will Waltz.

ISBN 979-8-9873662-1-9

This book is for her ear,
if she will wear it

PALE TO

PALE TO

PALE TO

PALE TO

PALE TO

WNIE

WNIE

WNIE

WNIE

WNIE

BY TOM WILL
BY TOM WILL
BY TOM WILL
BY TOM WILL
BY TOM WILL
BY TOM WILL
BY TOM WILL
BY TOM WILL
BY TOM WILL
BY TOM WILL
BY TOM WILL
BY TOM WILL
BY TOM WILL
BY TOM WILL
BY TOM WILL
BY TOM WILL
BY TOM WILL
BY TOM WILL
BY TOM WILL
BY TOM WILL
BY TOM WILL
BY TOM WILL
BY TOM WILL
BY TOM WILL

I would like this to be like an interview after some sporting event, but more to my preference. The interviewer always asks something the athlete does not want to, or does not know how to answer. But Tom, how does it feel to have completed *Pale Townie*? What emotions must be running through your mind right now? Imagine being asked that.

I would much rather, like the athlete, prefer to be asked a question that would make me "fall in" to an almost somnambulant recall of a more relevant, more practical issue that I am more willing and more able to talk about. How did you do it, Tom, and how did it come about?

Well it was the fallish late summer of 2022. I had just finished a first attempt at a collection which I was calling at the time *Sonnets, Gifts, and Sketches*, which I had undertaken to complete (or so I thought; I am still editing this collection at the time of writing this introduction) by driving 6 hours to the cheapest motel I could find in West Virginia, in a football town during an away game weekend, and editing the manuscript on printer paper with a pen at my room's large old desk. The motel was in some disrepair, with only a few rooms populated, namely the room directly to the right of mine, lived in by a kind talkative old woman from Columbia who kept her door open for her one-eyed kitten to come and go as he pleased, and also in her room she kept a large cage of several white doves. All the talking we did and I unfortunately never got a hold on the dove question, on how her doves came about, which I feel was a very important how question and still is.

Next thing I know and I was home again with a collection finished, if only in my mind for the moment. That left me with three collections, two published earlier in the year of 2022, and one, as I've said, more or less in the can as they say in Hollywood. The poetic vein felt plumbed in terms of what I was saying and how I was saying it. *Rocky 5*, *Dirty Harry 4*, *Tom Will 3*. Where to go next, what to say?

And then a gap in my memory. Although this was all only a few months prior (today is January of 2023 as I write this introduction) I do not exactly remember what possessed me to begin *Pale Townie*. Or to put it more mysteriously: I do not exactly remember what possessed me to attempt to rewrite the 999 line poem from Vladimir Nabokov's novel *Pale Fire*, retaining the novel poet John Shade's end rhymes; and then repopulating said end rhymes with new heroic couplets of my own design. But much like the writing of poetry, at a certain point in time you cannot remember not doing it. I am afraid the why was lost to the question somewhere in these bounds as well.

So it was that I was already a few weeks into my undertaking of *PT*. I was doing it. And this how I can now answer with great ease. I would come home from work, and write a stanza or two, fiddle with it somewhat, and then count how many lines I still have to go (this ritual, like the weighing of gold dust at the end of each day in *The Treasure of The Sierra Madre*, was an incredibly rich reward). This formula, giving allowances for breaks, weekends, holidays, and gushers of great poetic inspiration etc. I followed quite consistently. If there were ever any times when I felt especially lost I would simply refer to my source; how did John Shade handle this particular end rhyme, when did he enjamb, when did he ceasure, and so on. I simply and gradually followed my formula until mid-December, when I completed the fourth and final canto on the week of Christmas.

So there is how.

But how does it feel? The intrepid reporter angling in for a better line of attack. Well, I am not quite sure. On one hand I would like to borrow a line from a fellow introductory section to a fellow book of poetry. The book of poetry in question is Jack Spicer's *After Lorca*, a collection in which Jack faithfully translates several poems of Federico Garcia Lorca, Jack even seeing fit to add and omit the words and poems that Lorca forgot to add and omit himself. Interestingly enough, the introduction to Jack's book was written by the dead poet Lorca himself, and from this I quote for my own purposes:

"Frankly I was quite surprised when Mr. Spicer asked me to write an introduction to this volume. My reaction to the manuscript... was and is fundamentally unsympathetic. It seems to me the waste of a considerable talent on something which is not worth doing. However, I have been removed from all contact with poetry for the last twenty years. The younger generation of poets may view with pleasure Mr. Spicer's execution of what seems to me a difficult and unrewarding task."

Feeling pound for pound a stranger on the outside of our *Pale Townie*, who is himself a shade of John Shade, who too is a shade of the beloved V. Nabokov, thereupon removed I stand observant. And from this vantage I can only hope that a generation of younger poets(a horrifying phrase that conjures up images of campus cafeterium) finds some pleasure or some use for the 999 lines of the poem in this book.

On the other hand I would like to say that I think this is the best thing I have ever written, and I feel I can convince myself on a clear day that I am talking with several poets whom I have always been grateful to merely listen to. But I may go out tomorrow for a smoke, sit on my apartment building's covered stoop, and the color and temperature of the weather may cast me down into the sharp spikes for no reason at all. Regardless I feel secure in my folly because who would be foolish enough to follow me here?

On a third vestigial hand I feel that *Pale Townie* is not yet complete, because as we all know VN's *PF* was a book of four parts of equal necessity: introduction poem commentary index. Perhaps one fine day.

CANTO ONE

¹ I was the shadow of the townie slain
   Through my glasses and then the windowpane
   The changing light created new focus; I
   Lean convinced of death on the morning sky
   And sill; these glasses seem to duplicate
   The townie's death onto two bowling plates
   The thin unwound guitar strings made of glass
   The laminated bookshelves' tufted grass
   I refused to kill myself so the snow
¹⁰ Murdered me; sing muse of the weekend so
   Long and the death of your favorite son; stand
   Above me glasses; fly awhile don't land

   Next morning you woke to a frosted flake
   Of a townie in milk of frosted opaque
   While outside the sun was melting the white
   And licking tears of the snowblind with light
   And the car too cried itself back to blue
   On the dash sunglasses folded away a view
   Of ten thousandth commute ten thousandth frost
²⁰ As many cigarettes lit as children crossed
   I was late for work and skidded offroad
   With each tree my sanity tapped out a code
   To someone; and somewhere I dared repeat
   The code like when children dance on your feet
   Or when you stopped and let pass a family of grouse
   Or when you drove all night to see lights in a house
   All these tracks are fading on our lawn whose
   Mudroom cries with the policed sounds of shoes

   All liquors made me happy even Grey
³⁰ Goose; all bartenders loved me and so they
   Would let me write poems without a permit
   Or refill; I had a bookbag and it

1

Contained multitudes and undertable dwelt
My lighters my flasks my pencilbox svelte
My soul too from one flask dripped stillicide
To floors my friends; and just to the side
Of my seat a drinkring's dream which you too
Could finger when I leave; and if I do
Flank my eyes with two beers colored like leaves
40 Then the bar'll be shingled with poems for eaves

And my poems back then were leaves on the lake
That drank and drowned with too much to take
On; thank God they cut down every tree
And no one steps on my anything; see
How quiet and dunelike this treeless space
Has become in winter when you displace
The trees from the lake; now just snow between
The lake my old self and grass likely still green

50 I had a great fuck under a tree there
When I first a townie and they a spare
Calendar in a tire's inner sun
Long there; the rope of obscure knots undone
By the sudden weight of twelve girls all fell
And from then on I knew gravity well
It is murder and not a suicide; they
Killed me from outside myself; see I sway
As if pushed on that ropeswing; I swing

Like my glasses in pity taking wing
Married my shoulder blades as that's where there's
60 Rooms for wings of all sorts; guitars or chairs
Or birds or moths or of ropeswings instead
Of any angel's cloths; all visited
Me and ministered to my mockingbird
Heart; and somehow the mockingbirds had heard
Of me my pitiable wings; they flew clear

Through snowy night to see me lying here
Dead as a windshield when a bird flew aloft
Hit me and flew on; my windshield's grown soft
As mineral glass the townie cries; we
70 Like prey in a nature show on tv

I will be the scene where the franchise died
A sixth *Dirty Harry* was never tried
And no one knows what the odds are today
My guess is Clint is no Pale Townie; they
Let us age and tan and hairline recede
In the obvious direction; I read
These fifty or so lines and they refer
To only my limits; but to kiss her

Is without limits; her eyes brown nests
80 Her blue dress eggshells as fragile as guests
Fuck in a guestroom; quiet as a maid
Loud as a heart attack for hearts; I prayed
To her like only a townie can; well
I tried to but I mostly failed adul-
Lation; most nights my voice cracks eggs for God

Breakfast nowdays for townies is postmod-
Ern; the world stopped caring about my taste
Buds; the sandless beach is only interlaced
With rocks to eat; it's not my tune; doom
90 Is my doom no more; I enter my room
My room no more; the realtors will create
I create no more; eyes a paperweight
For my poems; my ashtray a lagoon
For my windows; tonight the townie moon
Will sing at beach parties like a guitar
Youngest brother will gaze to townie star
I asked you if what's on this cracker's for
Eating; the townie slept drunk at some door

3

In meeting the youngest brothers I've found
100 A confidence of birth that's not unsound
Of which I the blest eldest was born free
First born townie from first born townie me
I've inherited the joy of cheap coffee's taste
The freshly opened joy of canned coffee paste

Cheap coffee gives new pages color and age
No chance the pages or birds leave the cage
No chance the birds or earth 'scapes the sun
God let me though be a phenomenon
Of escape; make the bird and earth fly strange
110 As flapping glasses or gulls cross the range
Let them all like me slip their natural form
No matter how predictably the storm
Rages; reveal the curtain of your staged
Play at its edges; give clues that we're caged

Let iambs scale the pentameter wall
And let pentatonic scales on eyes fall
Like glazed milk; some townie preached upon hill
Alone like one vibrato spring I trill
In the floating bridge; the windows will bear
120 All things in patience like my callouses were
Touch them in death to write something; no sand
In case of blizzards; if the poem and
The townie can be explained than I'll head
Uphill to write a new one; or I'm dead

My death cannot be explained I daresay
But can explain; think of it in this way
Not things into words; Williams alive now
But words into things will blow me through bough
To prove the unseen wind; you praised me fat
130 With those words; I a simple flapping bat

I was the shadow of the townie slain
Falling asleep against the windowpane
When I need you; where are you my unique
Friends I need you now; circus geek and freak
Close in; paste and feather and cowboy chaps
They mean to camp me up in death; perhaps
An open casket; glitter has not left
Me alone in death; see it fall as deft
As undertaker's dandruff falls on pain
140 And death camps out outside my house again
Tonight and every night there is no day
I can't shake off the poem's glitter as I lay
Death still the forest glitters like a toy
My bloodless head pale as an altar boy
With locked knees; I dreamt this besides the bed
Then winked to get the blood back in my head

Just yesterday I creaked the floors sublime
When I awoke and dressed for the last time
And cracked the knuckles on my poem's hand
150 And coffee played along my spinal strand
Like stoic Hemingway backpacked through Spain
Before then we both knew he'd blown his brain
Knew years ago when coffee beans were green
And shook on it before the Pleistocene
And agreed on shotgun and on window stone
As drinks of choice to cleave our townie bone

I got so grim speaking this afternoon
Of death he tried to take my weekend's swoon
But for townies death is a weekend's dim
160 Sunglasses pair; one eye's sky; one's a swim
And the wire frame's a long waisted wench
That joins twisting airs to waters that quench
Me like a fish; forever I'm allured
Forever sick town and forever cured

Forever I lean dead on windowpanes
My glasses on the dashboard still remains

CANTO TWO

Now dead; I'm driven as I was in my youth
From the limo's third row I squint out at truth
Driving by; I'll try and count these few known
170 Things; in the limo the townie alone
Must regard speed as some conspiracy
With death's tinted windows to obscure me

For this world too has made a ghost of doubt
Within me and tints all outside without
Discrimination; half awake through doom
I drive away slow; roll away the tomb

God damned my eyes; this landscape is not night
It only appears so; why bother fight
God; two rams are slain under the abyss
180 Of an overpass; the Greek first drinks this
The blood like cardinals below waxwings
In overpass trees; Tiresias sings

"Where are you going where are where are
You going; where are you going you star
With no constellation; without a pair
Of glasses townie; and are you aware
Of the landscape or of just your thumb
Where are you going you foolish you glum
Townie; crying because the song is blue
190 Like some song sang to you when you were new
This is not your mother's song; so don't flirt
And hide behind juvenilia's skirt
Where are you going townie; thumb so thin
Yet all he sees is his own dumb skin"

This song only served to increase my hush
As the blood left the birds and faces grew flush

Adam and Eve drank; blood scent to them a sail
That dead sharks found under highway's dale
200 Where ivy won't grow; where leaves only sit
On breast and waist; no wine of Christ has lit
Their eyes; as they lay on town's naked wrist
Adam and Eve then sang in the blood mist
"Oh they're ain't no thing in this world I've found
To replace my lover's sweet sleeping sound
Oh there ain't a bite in this world I've took
That I wouldn't spit out for my love's look
Oh there ain't no death in this life in vain
If it's your sweetheart that blows out your brain"

Their harmony without a third; decay
210 Was theirs again; God ignored them that day
Then; he never bought their full length tape
So false to him; it only feigned escape
At this I did not sing your song and I
Regret my weakness; but should you die
One day how could I keep quote un quote time
And then stomach's shock as if pre-song; I'm
Imagining that you had died and had
Approached the car-bright blood and eyelids mad
With blood mascara; your cratered palms weird
220 From pavement pebbles; could God have appeared

Why a townie would wonder all this; why
In life or death care what will not verify
Itself; it seems the blood during my talks
Has seeped inside my shoes; and in my walks
To and fro inside my tint of mind my wings
Like car upholstery in shade tipped things
Back to unwinged mind; cigarettes in dream
Colors; tans and creams these wings of mine seem
To have gotten drunk off ram's blood; now most
230 Of all I wish to fly to you as a ghost

Let us both verify and then translate
I dead you alive the pleasures of fate
Fly to you each night to feel how terse
My wings with lust; no time for townie verse

Lost in thoughts of bee wings drenched in the dark
Below the overpass; the muffled bark
Of blood drinking faded; a Frenchman died
In '78; custard beaten; eyed
Me; his neck had a noose and his arm a piece
240 Of chair; both loosed after the miles from Nice
Jacob Brel spoke like Esau; "*Je nourris*"
And he waited; that was his song; and he
Sang it; the French have always been not wrong
Not right; but throats and asses for my song

Just so Melville was best as he could hear
And see the yankee dream and sang it dear

I did not forget *Magnet of Doom*; knew
You knew I he knew all American U-
Niversity towns well; I without class
250 Forget the dead have no films only grass
But I an American as was discussed
And we impossibly shoot films from dust
Unlikely this too; I here so reclined
Driving to my death; vow not to fall behind
Til cameras run out of film in my head
I'll still love tint and gauze and the spread
Of light on lenses polished like the stone
That made the knife that cut my thousandth bone
In two; all these cannisters are with me
260 In the limo dark; clear as ice in tea

I've learned by now the fruit sharpens the teeth
The knife the stone; the bird the car beneath

Just so in limo we've laid the rams down
And drive on; laid in trunk to bleed it brown
My wings out the windows; I am the nape
Of the carneck in hood ornament shape
Sharpening the air and light I cut all
As death sharpens rocks with its waterfall

And in this way was I drove and caressed
270 And many poems with my wing were blest
Many obscure things the car did explain
And many poets struck in oncoming lane
Or flung far right under blood's sudden shade
Your poems and mine all kissed townie's blade

The limo's an altar for rams; the least
Fleeced sang the loudest yet were the least creased
The townies too are the sheep sounds of times
Not as far off as you'd admit; our chimes
Rev somewhere most nights but chime now no more
280 And now we've arrived in front of my door

Oh God God; nobody has shoveled the lawn
I realize that until this task is gone
And thousands more; I'll have nothing but this
House and no heaven; no coffee no kiss
Only a limo's tint that can't admire
Itself; until someone inspects the fire-
Place; defrosts the fridge; checks battery pack
Cleans behind the sink's mountain range; throws sack
After sack of insulation out the most
290 Small attic window I'm a townie ghost
A ram; a chime; no just me as I look
And cry; my house lives on much like my book

A family may move in and add to blend
Another patch of cloth that death will rend

And quilt to me; this house can barely say
Another word should deeper fugue inveigh
Against itself another pipe and slight
The organ; the harmony is now quite
Above; after four voices will assuage
300 Any further voices; and in this age
How many in many voices will say
None to none and in cathedral play
Too high or low in trees as rotting fruit
And who will circle this verse and say "cute"

The battle never fought lies never won
Now my house will symbolize decay's fun
Stretched across my skin to remove all doubt
Carpenter bees climb in to pull me out
As from a caved in mine from early age
310 When townies acted far below the stage
And in their turns the birds would pantomime
The miner's death in caged but human time
The birds like clocks would chime with one fell broom
A watch's jewel lies still in one small room

Jewels pin the cheap earth from spinning away
And depending on embargoes they may
Number few; friction has not much burned
Them in the furnace but still have turned
Them over with curious female voice
320 Again; again the spinning jewels rejoice
As men while cheaper steel would overstress
Again; again the townie licks the mess
And presses birds of paradise in books
Again the world hides in the watch's looks
I hold the motion of the moon phase still
I hold your wrist close as we climbed the hill
Your jewel-pin cut my throat and when I spoke
The moon was hidden in the mountain smoke

And so I took you to the miners' ball
330 Beneath the ground and lanterns swayed the hall
Pale townie fire swung from lanterns great
And to and fro their moonlight's swinging gate
Caught up the eye of every miner's beau
The chronographic moons all wound to go
Then stop; the earth the moon the stars the dance
When morning came we fed Proust's dog in France

Who barked out all my sins and my defeats
Soon every dog in France was in the streets
Knew all my poems' faults as if they sit
340 Listening under critics' chairs; when they knit
Their wires crossed the day wakes up real nice
No radio but barking dogs for twice
Blessed Orpheus; sung with his eyes of course
And birds with fingers; France forgive the force
On your slim wrists as I drag you through nights
Of a townie drunk under city lights
Cocteau; Renoir; I wish your songs could top
The modern charts instead of dog's doo-wop
To wear Dubois on wrist; a katydid
350 That green grin in French-*Casablanca* did
Me and Charlie in; who can criticize
Her screen test when the curses light her eyes
Who can curse French dogs or Proust in his bed
I've always bruised things rolling in my head
These thoughts below a dogging neighbor's moan
A ball bounced off the wall in monotone

God; get me out of France I'm too morose
I have only strength now to dream of those
Eighties' Belmondo flicks where that dog played
360 A killer of Africans and women made
To look so with fake tan; how he smiled
While killing mercenaries oh so mild

Imagine if he wrote Death of the Text
And was the French philosopher to next
Sign that child fucking petition; be
Still Belmondo; Denevue awaits and me
And Varda cums to you as she did then
Thank God you chose the gun and not the pen

I watched *One Hundred and One Nights* again
370 And cried the week I died; hard to explain
What happens when the screen tints tangerine
And girls read books to me in bed I mean
They read my books to aged me and roar
In my ear "*oh la lune en cuir; j'adore*"

Suddenly the meanings change; now they read
My book through false eyelashes; all is said
In judgment; each poem a cold document
Then sobbing witness whose meanings meant
Different things at different times; your eyes three
380 Beautiful colors whisper back at me
As they judge the eyelashes of my play
Maybe in death or France I'll find a stay

Please note my eyes in death show signs of hope

When I was twelve and looking for the pope
I'm always twelve; especially on that day
I the youngest monk; the abbot's fiancé
Was not born yet; but then the papal car
Taught me techniques for drinking at the bar
Alone and looking up and vaguely past
390 The wall; I the contractor gives the last
But fairest estimate; I the dour dean
The carpenter pencil that kept streets clean
With knife bright eyes as good for cleaning chum
As paring nails; but then the pope has come

And gone; my hope is still not understood
Had he not come how long could I have stood
By now the abbot's lost it all awhile
But surely he must still think back and smile
From cell to cell; which one did he prefer
400 The spirit or the wife; which one was her
With launching eyes; and which was just instead
A boat gone laughing off to loch and head

I was almost Frank Stanford at fifteen
I was discerning as running through screen
Doors; I saw him through the twilight headstone's blur
Read Dickinson then but I didn't like her
How could I hide away a cassocked jane

How could I read or write if stuck in Maine
Who only had some pork and beans for wars
410 The townie's silent film shown before bores
The General speeds me on; beyond debate
The bridge on stilted fire; 6…7…8…
The fire's crash is pale in black and white
And it enjambed by chance a young fawn's rite
Who saw the dream accordion in the wood
And saw the dream enjamb his song; still stood
The steam ship whistle lingering still in proof
As Vlad-mir tossed the poets from its roof
So the fawn learned steampipes too could sing
420 And as the fire cooled his organs ring
You know the rest; you've heard a mouth harp call
You've seen a wet deck shuffled; seen a hall
Ambush set by *It's Your Life Post-Fame*
And Donald O almost forgot your name
You built a house but no one was behind
It when it fell; forgive my townie mind
That pun; like others I just had to know
The feel; crashing your car spending your dough

The phrenology of that travelog
430 Part jew part ape; I rent from him in fog
That never cleared; a train cries from afar
I never learned its schedule or the star
To sail her by; the fog is like the sea
And we three bobbing lures in it; all three
Of us dead; homeowner her and me; all
Stars flying door to door in the recall
Something else I never learned; lines are light
And shadow; black landlords vote white and white
Landlords vote black; how usura in red
440 Walked; high heels on the roof; baked Pound his bread
Charged him interest; Stanford too sang loud
In his uncollected works of that same crowd
That captured my youth; and the floating door
Opens for a God; and his leopards floor
The wood with carpet paws and altar sense
And grapevines crawled likes cats along the fence
I ask the fog; when will we be unmasked

Mr. Poem answers any questions asked
Who won this year's cup; in football of course?
450 How can he answer all without remorse?
Yet never forget his tranquility?
Who took my photo under the marquee?
Why in death do poems read like inane
Lists? What is the price of futures in grain?
What cures pox in chickens? Gallicism
Rhymes with what? Who framed the photo? Prism
Killed who in the Iliad? What was said?
Who took my scissors to the picture's head?
And where is the neck from which it once peered?
460 Answer; in the poem's fog; disappeared

I love *The 39 Steps* because that
Was the film best to wed without a chat

Man to woman handcuffed and unafraid
Of the key; as a blackface band played
Jazz you spun to me; the camera's eye tricked
And free; like knitting needles we both flicked
And stabbed; and on Saturdays we'd go out
Naked and keep our cuffed arms still about
The moor; between us both our clothes dried quick
470 You'd need binoculars to learn that trick
Another; on Sundays as was the law
We cooked outside; and then you would have saw
Us arm in arm reach through a fire's black

But were not burned; that shack is not this shack
That foggish moor did not have this fog's bent
The tan lines gone; the cuffs resized they went
As wedding gifts when we were running late

In death my poems are just a clay plate
To me; pull gone; pull gone; shuck shells and throw
480 More in; pull throw; pull throw; and now I know
My song; I only ever hear the clock
At night; now the fog freezes into rock

I freeze along; but when today was young
And I commuted home with death I flung
And flew in hope; I thought that you showed
Up in the lean of every pole; in every road
Unturned; I failed the test and the retake

Unallowed in death; the ivy on the lake
Shore after many hellish years uncrossed
490 Now coats the lake floor frozen under frost
And there I sing my song the shell-same way
Today; is this the song betrayers say
Another remade film I know I know

Cocteau; my camera died my circuits blow
My poems skating live until the spring
I get all my ideas from their shivering
Brief lines; the limo sunk below the ground
Through tint and darkly ice I am still drowned
Another chore; trim the ivy from the bank
500 Or climb down the rope to find me where I sank

CANTO THREE

Only a monk could be a Rabelais
Just so only a townie can now lay
In the filth of a lake in spring; the P
Of lures descends like papal rings and we
Mutely kiss at spring; Easter came to term
And is that your earring that hangs a worm
It looks like yours and so I bite as I

Bit before; the worm left for limo's wye
Dash oak appointments; was this Dante's state
510 When gravity reversed and Lethe's gate
In greeting hummed; left Satan weeping there
Below their feet a worm frozen in fair
Punishment; God please be fair to me if
I try again; your earring be my glyph

It grows on my tongue like a violet
A lily; an opal's bad luck and yet
Do you remember dear when you first missed
It; in death the townie is a preterist
Of all our sex that still in memory thrives
520 This earring was lost early in our lives
A Friday 'round 5 in Hollywood piles
Of papers; you'd stayed to help with the files
And how lonely was that lone floweret
Like Jesus Christ for all weekend; forget
Him not; forget all your earrings unless
Him; I know your lobe in its tenderness
Your shoes soled in jewels for the unique pain
Some people spend a whole weekend on a plane
So why should not a townie cause dismay
530 And rise from the dead in such casual way
And arrive maybe in Indochinese slime
Like Dante passing through the earth in rhyme

The Chinese townie would likely be banned
Or cut off his tongue's flowering ampersand
The preterist faith is useless when dead
Good news for the Jews in limbo instead

"My daughter" cars cried and thought me unwise
As I carried your ring to paradise
Walking down the highway I sang "hullo"
And walked by a guardrail that only shrugged "no"
540 But I took his photograph his hair tossed
Under snow and bent from a crash long lost
To the road; the earring and I alone
A new song; the earring and I unknown
And Adam and Eve; oh woah may putresce
But who can miss them when you wore that dress
I write best when jumping on the roadside bed
A fresh snow grows on the guardrail's bent head

The earring was a P and &; now G
550 A wonderful utility; the debris
Swirls like conventioneers giving dancers tips
The P and G powerlines shall eclipse
Me for miles more; so I'm not a ghost
I'm not the humming lines' song; they sing "coast
To coast; coast to coast; coast to coast; coursed through
Like wine"; the strippers in the bathroom; you
Lost track of time; the powerlines still gasp
I left and walked on; the sky turning jasp
A dentist out front sang; "in outer space
560 For the night and the night is a briefcase
Of drugs; both disappear with the sun; do
You have a mouth; every girl has one; you
Are mouthfuls of girls"; he sang like a toad
This man crying behind me on the road
This out of towner sawing in the pine
Like Pilate washed his hands of the divine

Any poet that can't expect a change
In salary is half-mine; disarrange
Hartford Crane's job from his advice
570 And then Wallace Steamship would have jumped twice
A double indemnity; perhaps both
The poets would wrap twice like ivy growth
Round the ship's propeller; Pacific Life
And Risk won't insure the earring; my wife
She must have been the lady of the pond
Or some effect of sun had made her blonde
Hair trilene line and the poet a shade
Pale fish; and her earring our balustrade
Fell quietly as a flame's rising gaze
580 So you all reached me in the water's haze
An ivy townie wrapped round a plastic toy
If birth were a resurrection the boy
Would think of it often and give wild
Variants; so too I am a boy child
Was it dentists or Hartford men who bare
Their songs to me on the road; did I wear
The cast on the left leg; in any case
Before I jumped nobody saw my face

And now the strangest things are not so hard
590 To do; the house that I would disregard
I now paint ceaselessly to match that shame
Of fog and ivy and blood; and my same
Blood too; all droplets in the shaker's war
Every year a new aspect to my door
Is added; speckles light the townie gloom
The streets still look like searchlights from my room

The pocket's lip deepens your earring's call
And my ear too is nailed to the plaid wall
And swims drunk like a post game townie goon
600 I clean the ear; the earring; the baboon

Chime of a car; I cut the grass of us
The way I mow a lawn is calculus
That starts a family; if you'd discern
See the resurrected child soft as fern
And the sweat of grass and the laundry tied
Resurrection's miracle I deride
Compared to a child; I have not spit
Like a child; my poem less than it

Can learn; less than child's spittle is man
⁶¹⁰ Still with spit I clean the dust from the fan
I clean the purgatory from the night
I clean the stigmatized house of blood light
I clean the iodized arms of its spilled past
I clean each cut blade of grass; all dreams fast
I clean townie teeth of its whiskey tongues
I clean the nicotine from townie lungs

I am a child how the wed foresee
It on their wedding day; the great maybe
Of what's possible; see me in their eye

⁶²⁰ And all other eyes there; so my life by
Death is a wedding where all eyes tell
Of me; see also this in Lewis' hell

By bus tour; see the divorced townies snort
The murderer and the murdered scouse retort
At angels; his heaven makes many wraiths
But this townie is living out other faiths
Of latticed hell and heaven; both a role
Just so two sinners can make one new soul
They can make heaven; but enough Chinese
⁶³⁰ I'd rather death himself to the foul teas
Of a manifesto and those that go
By and for them; rather be a jingling Poe

Or cousin to Jerry Lee Lewis' strange
Blood; or a family of six at the range
And I a twenty-two; a fat kneed priest
On my kneeler; my heresy at least
Can be blamed on the brand of fishing line

Or Remington's production in decline
Or Lee Poe's nursery rhyme made to take in
⁶⁴⁰ Some young Alice; or the small mandolin
Strings to my fingers; or cousins inept
As the shell's misfire that one day crept
Or the confessional's unlabeled womb
Or the fishing line still snagged on my tomb

So too the limo and hearse are in their way
Heaven and hell; and both waiting survey
The world with lidless eyes like a child
Surveys a book of poems backwards; styled
Like day and night and day and night in wood
⁶⁵⁰ The forest drives away; the windowed tint would
Not roll down at first; then obeying me
The lake water pours out and drinks the tree

This is someone's creation myth I hear
You broke my will like strings it thrills me dear

Goodness gracious; trees in water and light
Taught us where the roots could be found allright

Mama play that that's alright song again
The trees all on stilts in my windowpane

The giants on stilts and barely the thud
⁶⁶⁰ Of the primeval bow-tight draw of mud

No stones no rain no sound no way is pinned

The delta frogs are louder than the wind
Of a hurricane; I'm in the wild
Untaught guitar of a lonely child

Here I stay; and where you stay til the last
And others come and go from that place fast
That is your town and you its townie; run
To the hardware store for chains; if the sun
Goes stay; I like this too; if the leaves brown
670 Stay; if the electorate of your town
Should change; if its liquor laws be re-tamed
And taxes written by that damn acclaimed
Poet; stay; if the year might change each year
And the house inflates with memory; where
Boulders stay; stay; where no leaves touch the stream
I stay; if one of mine stays in the dream
It ceases to be their hurricane; on
The boardwalk of dreams stay; so what if Donne
Went over; so what if the hurricane
680 Won an award and went to school in Maine
Everywhere I go I have stayed and spied
It all; to have stayed is not to have died

Et all; let us take up brush and discuss
Impasto; the brush stays; then there is us
And then we fade but what remains; short
Or long the brush; the bubbling lines the thwart
Of naked trees beyond the color's end
The leaves have left; but the townie will attend
To the brush strokes of all trees; disagree
690 And you'll die; but not Wayne Thiebaud and me

The ego swells within the poem's trance
The star expands in silence at the chance
To swallow more; the tugging at the feet
Of one more townie; all strings down beat

At once; just one more toe to go before
The kettle drums; the mallet of one more
Silent constellation smashed; the bear now
In his trap; the drums ring gong-like and how
And now he implodes, the river once crossed
700 Is never crossed again; pray for the lost
Townies and their implosions; the regret
Shrunk down into marbles that now down set
Have the weight of dead universes; spin
And roll in death; the drugs swirl within
The bag of damned and saved lives interlinked
Save me; this townie's requiem's distinct
My death writes what my resurrection's played

The earring is now the requiem made
In D; or concerto twenty behind
710 The piano; a finger trap of mind
In D; my stuck fingertips recognize
Your ears' insides as easily as eyes
The lobe; I walk to you to see the twig
Your stirring ear that in my hands feels big
Every tree an imagined ear in case
I never see yours again; I replace
Your body around the earring; your felt
Lobe your pool hall desire your chalk dwelt
On like palms like the tree bark of some stray

720 Your eyes are still so many miles away
But I collect them; they fall to earth
Each night; any star patch has your eyes' mirth
And in the center of the earth no state
Of hell but your lips I hallucinate
Their smile and bite; and tonight perhaps
Is a clear night and when your eyes collapse
Past the horizon I will walk on half-dead
To you once more to see what you have said

Another complication for the wrist kept
⁷³⁰ Watch; the movement of her breasts that quick stepped
Over the wire fences guarding hot
Concrete vats of oil the searchlight not
Catching us fuck besides the highway pipe
Line; somewhere in the warm northwest night; ripe
To touch we touched and now I walk the part
Of dreams; far off as a powerline's heart

Her body still dreaming; the stone white tone
Of a modern museum with its own
Rooms of Twombly Thiebaud and Rothko on
⁷⁴⁰ Walls white as cakes; the whole place from her; shone
Out from her like from a holy tent's glare
At night the waist of her corridor there
Is lit up and thin and waiting and stood
Still in lights as white as naked birch wood
In snow; a half-ghost cased the building one day
And that night drifts clear white though the display

I was not struck by just one magazine
But by the entire stand; I have been
Reading page by page in search of her hand
⁷⁵⁰ And none are even her finger or land
That she has touched; what then has wind contained
The Ellis Island of the damned page; stained
With ink the townie walks and has no choice
But to wish for a car to toss the voice
Of masses into pits of tar remote
As those in wastrel's hell; to see some quote
Of these bad poets burn in her through smoke
As I found her in the song; I awoke

My townie wings like the left hand of Schmidt
⁷⁶⁰ Began to play and the air under it
Listened; the wings as still as what John Smith

Saw; and the air the new world; stirring myth
Of reeds; now lightpoles are reeds; now the mark
Of the steel mill's foot now a river dark
With reeds; by air the wings feather each tooth
And above the reeds the mouth of wide truth

The whole world below me is just reeds; Jim
Bryant John Fahey and I sing to him
Hallowed townie hymns that once stalked past her
770 Window; the saints with flutes of reeds that purr
The slain rams asleep but listening rapt
As the earring in my pocket; though trapped

Is now complete as if all letters meet
Within it to preserve all of our sweet
Language; and now of course the townie tried
Some crass joke between the hymns; an aside
Up here is welcome as a journalist
In the primum mobile; and they insist
With reedlike insistence that I'm not all
780 Together ready to respond or call
And wings move aside as I fall to you
In cool rushes of reedlike wings; I review
The sunrise from a plane's height like a niece
At a reunion; the music a piece
Of slow pulses of peace from death; I sense
A return to the cheap smoke of the dense

Perhaps it was the pale earring which might
Have dragged me back to life; now the letter's white
Fire waits to inscribe your dark hair's veil
790 Our earring of secret language; detail
By detail of my death and life all fond
And superimposed in this townie bond
To be worn by you townie's town and me
When we three visit the lake let it be

Like visiting a graveyard's grassy brink
At first avoided and then we don't think
And walk on the grass; the flat stones low coats
All gathered like at a stoning; Paul notes
The way Stephen saw heaven then died; file
800 Me by him; please me by him; style
Me much like him; I saw heaven and much
Like Stephen I was thrown with a stone's touch

I died saw heaven's reeds and the misprint
Corrected by the next Monday; a hint
Of my return in the local abyss
In a never solved crossword clue; "if this
Poet lives then he kept to a theme
Finally; and if it was not a dream
Then it is not a mere coincidence
810 That his name has a sentence's brief sense
Terse in English; smooth yet possible; find
Him in a dead man's drawer; or a kind
Of Rudyard Kipling chore; or in a game
Of fools; but still he lives here all the same"
But thirty-one down has never been found

I woke up that Monday without a sound
But not from a dream but from my involute
Resurrection; I sprung coiled round mute
Obscurity and failure the sole pawns
820 Of my sanity; no more sense then Faun's
Falls; Young Girl's Run; the extinguishing
Freeway lights of exit signs; green linking
Every green name to the morning high-
Way; or guarding the obscure radar's sky
The array warms me; I've been cold as keys
And sure of radiation meant for these
Townie organs before; but these events
In my morning eyes hang as ornaments

In the cold ear of possibilities

830 You were as real as God and now it is
Moreso; I kiss the unlocked unpierced door
Of your ears; I kiss the reeds of your mouth more
Than Moses could his mother; then I grope
Back to work full anew of townie hope

CANTO FOUR

I the pale sugar that dissolves tea has
Drank now at the cupped air; I drink tea as
I dissolve this past weekend; its charm none
But its vague promise of what may be done
This is the same weakness as our machine
840 Of mind; but I've sharpened it in between
Two trees into a paler sweeter kind
Of bitter free that takes the clay of mind
And gives the chipping mug what only he
Distills; and if you planted grave flowers be
Not then sad; but drink now in still wilt; when
They touch me chastely in my sleeping pen

A poem is the backwards kind of thought
Of a crawfish dreaming; no waves are fought
No townie nets no dogs no dixie bar
850 Association moon or northern star
Or business cards; led by some asswards phrase
The crawfish swims backwards throughout my maze

And wakes up in my pot; so then the brain
That was not in use dissolves and no pain
Like tea in sugar; I age like the drill
Battery; about half an hour of will
Until resurrection's automaton
Cuckoo clock figurine won't switch back on
Then in waking erect I pass the store
860 Window; and the maid blushes as before

I dissolve the maid; she blushed because
She saw my charm before the battery's pause
And now on the bottle's label for all time
She blushes at my resolve; and the rhyme
Of the poem is the two focused eyes

Of a newton's cradle that tries and tries
To knock the poem off the conscious desk
And makes my townie rhythm poetesque
A hammer's strike will always rhyme; and when
870 The hammer's grip dissolves into a pen
The paper sugar white at my command
Dissolves the job and desk and townie hand

If you could see my townie back preferred
Within slouch; and if you had overheard
The nitrogen strikes rolling around me
As I stretch a storm dissolves into free
And distant regions; then you'd see the lawn
Like God; and each lightning would be a dawn
Of new townie life; each hailstone a shoe
880 So small it melts ever smaller into
Shoeless blades of grass; and then struck awoke
By thunder and moving farther off it broke
Dissolved; into the sea then me; my damp
Is where the sea and grey horizon stamp
And meet like lovers; then dissolve inborn
Within each other; the foggy chalk of morn
Is my sugar that hovers in their staid
Morning; and enjambment is the grey shade
Of clouds at sea; and caesura a sort
890 Of gutter to avoid ends; the support
Of my angel keeps my heart in its place
In reed fields hunting; it's so hard to face
What the cloud's end means for me; that he'd
Be dissolved and we would finally bleed

All this on my commute lays on my skin
Like aspirin drops fed to a heart's thin
Apple crust; shaving a candle's sugar wick
Like a docked ship to one day in the nick
Of time sail an escape; the cool and free

⁹⁰⁰ Apple pie hangs in breeze and smells to me
   Like a church; still I go work; still a pear
   Hurts my teeth; still the pie staves off despair
   When it peals in the church steeple at eight
   PM in prayer; still I palpitate
   Still I shake an aspirin bottle's mess
   Of sound; oh death where is thy prickliness

   Like the thus spoke the Persian German bloke
   I commute down the mountain with a two-stroke
   Engine and overhear a pope; his chin
⁹¹⁰ Sang "archives of despair cabinets of skin
   Priests wrote down all your sins; them bimanists
   One hand blesses and that right hand assists
   But the leftmost hand lists; so sinner dance
   The lowliest angel knows your cock's each stance"

   We listed down the hill two trails of soap
   I heard he's no longer a pope; I hope
   His naked head stays warm; one time a blaze
   Of thorns I wore; a penitent country phase
   I remember the color but I'll send
⁹²⁰ Away for just the feel of one thorn's end
   Of green graded into brown in a scheme
   Of simplicity which burnt away to cream

   As a bonfire burns as it always has
   The townie semicolon sounds like jazz
   With a black fingertip and a valve of black
   A hammer's handle burnt off; bricabrac
   Across the mountainside burns where whole schools
   Of jazz are burning; dance hall, school hall; pools
   Of it burning; Mungus by the damned Marx
⁹³⁰ Semicolons circle my head; like sharks

It will end like knee deep in the town's creek
With nothing left to say; like I'm a cheek
Of cold vibrating glass; the shore too steep
For rabbits; like window vibrations creep
In and say nothing's left to say; but now
And then a car misses the bridge to plough
Into my river; like cocks the car grows
In slow motion and knee deep splashes my nose

It will end like a bottle of abstruse
940 Liquor evaporated from no use

It will end; and like a radio's roam
From point to point; my omnipotent comb
At nothing's throat; it will end like a spoon
At a full breast; the office's afternoon
It will end like a toothache; like I dine
That is with my eye on what is not mine
Like the empty cop car waits; everywhere
It ends like how girls share a single chair

It seems to end like many things I love
950 Begin; and so I boast of things above
Below and at town's equator; I stress
Resurrection is my boastful dress
Like Christ when he was behind the stone-caught
Tomb; knew the boulder's name its every thought
Its family town and architect; knew
That rolling tongue would boast of me and you

My townie sacrilege is not by rote
And no more than Stephen's; my scouts will float
Downstream on a raft of coats; a new term
960 For townie may arise but I won't squirm
Beneath another nail nor will I require
Any test beyond to start a fire

A collapsed bridge is a river sustained
By the millflame's prayer; a mountain drained
Of topmetals prays like Job; some tape meant
To keep the door unlocked; the bridge's cement
Stripped away in places kept the consonne
Onset and always rhymes; the star upon
The townsquare tree is a full moon unplanned
970 The businesses open late understand
It's Christmas; the vestments make plum a part
Of everyday life; the local on-sale art
Is yarn-stringed guitars; the man's delight
At his wife warm in bed sleeps to her right
The one snowplow in town becomes divine
And re-sanguinates twice a year; the line
It plows in the key of G; boats survive
All winter somehow; the strays keep alive
On driftwood from warmer climes; you and I
980 Take up ham radio and call July
I hit all spares; I first roll one then nine
Every single frame; I cough then I'm fine
My songs predict extensions of myself
Already two new stockings on the shelf

And whatever color the cover attains
Thank you; take a cue from grey windowpanes
Thank you; could the song fade out; could 42
Pages be considered a life; thank you
Pages thank you life thank you book; I see
990 An asterisk in the tea like a tree
With one leaf; thank you leaf; the tree sings "clunk"
Thank you one leaf's part in felling the drunk
Thank you photo on the back with face banned
And blurred; I thank black and white photo's sand
A photo is taken once more in the white
Of the community enlarger's light
This is a photo taken again; butterfly

Thank you though I've not seen you in years; bye
And again thank you up and down my lane

APOCALYPSE
CONFIDENTIAL
IS

Jacob Everett..*Publisher & Editor-in-Chief*

Brendan McCauley...*Deputy Publisher*

Hermes S. Thurston...*Deputy Publisher*

Max Thrax..*Managing Editor*

Tom Will...*Poetry Editor*

D.A. Wohler...*Fiction Editor*

Tully K..*Editor-at-Large*

Will Waltz...*Books Editor*

FORTHCOMING TITLES
FROM
APOCALYPSE CONFIDENTIAL

Incurable Graphomania
by Anna Krivolapova

PREVIOUSLY
ON
APOCALYPSE CONFIDENTIAL

THE BOOK OF
BY FRANK PEAK